Brando's Golf Gadg

For Women

Bobbi – Hit 'em
long & straight
Davy

Sonoma Publishers

P. O. Box 6779, Santa Rosa CA 95406 (707-566-9776)
www.sonomapubs.com

Written by: Gary Brobst and Dan Frazier

Illustrations by: Dan Frazier, Shawn Lux, and Steven Fontaine

Creative Contributor: Chris Olsen

Cover Painting: Shawn Lux

ISBN   0 - 9709468 - 2 - 1
First Printing
Printed in Canada

Brando's Golf Gadgets:
For Women

Equipment to Beautify the Royal and Ancient Game

By Gary Brobst and Dan Frazier

Sonoma Publishers
Santa Rosa, California, United States of America

Brando's Golf Gadgets: *For Women*

Dedication

I don't remember what kind of ball I was playing. But.... I'm sure the one you found was mine.

- Gary

Contents

My name is Brando. I invent things. In my first book, *Brando's Golf Gadgets*, I revealed nine great inventions to shave strokes off your round of golf. So what if they didn't conform to those stuffy rules of the royal and ancient game.

While most of my golf gadgets are equally useful to men and women, it has been pointed out to me that women have their own unique golfing problems that would benefit greatly from my gadgetry expertise. Therefore, I focused my skills to solve some of those dilemmas that specifically affect the average woman golfer.

After significant research, I found there is no such thing as an average woman golfer. So, I decided to locate three women who best exemplified the various aspects of this great sport. But, where to look? Where could I go to find those who could truly appreciate my golf gadgets? Well, after only a few moments thought, the answer was obvious! The Glen Isle Royal Golf Course offers some of the most unique and interesting challenges in the world of golf today. Located on an island in the Florida Keys, designed by the famous Loon Johnson, this course has recently become popular among the more innovative of the golfing set. Setting out to Glen Isle to look for candidates for my Golf Gadgets for Women, I investigated the first spot one goes to check out a golfer's talents - the practice area.

The Practice Area

Some people say the practice area is not a place for competition. These are the same people who lose well and frequently to golfers who know better. The practice area is the ideal spot to make a strategic statement to someone you want for a partner, making that chip onto the phoney green or sinking the long twenty footer to impress them. If you don't have the skills to pull off feats such as these, show off your calm confidence by not practicing at all. (Thereby not revealing any weaknesses!) Personally, I prefer to mess up royally in the practice area, and then claim a high handicap when competition starts. Poor performance on the practice tee also earns great odds on bets made during the round. I selected my "three average women golfers" from their practice area routine and mannerisms. Let's see how these women shape up and get ready to play the royal and ancient game.

Jane "Loose Shoes" Smith

Jane loves the game of golf and everyone has fun playing a round with Jane. She is an elementary school teacher, grades 3-4, so her golf is restricted to weekends. She enjoys the chance to get some exercise and soak up the contact with nature that is denied her during the week. Jane is an amiable hacker (a whopping 25 handicap) who likes to get an edge on the competion, but isn't terribly upset by an occasional quadruple bogie. Occasionally she gets a good run of pars between her eights, surprising her opponents with wild powerful swings that have a decent amount of accuracy. These big swings help overcome her awful short game and have yielded two holes-in-one! Just for insurance, Jane starts every round with at least eight balls in her bag. Without a doubt, a few well placed golf gadgets will catapult Jane into a handicap that doesn't start with a 2.

Here's Jane's typical practice routine.

Jane's final warm-up swing is a French roast latte, half caf, with cinnamon powder, vanilla syrup shot, two packets of refined sugar, and a dash of Himalayan nutmeg. Now she's ready to go!

Kokie "Must Win" Jameson

Kokie Jameson has a legendary and well funded golf obsession. She is married to Joe Jameson, owner of the international Mac Dukles fast food chain. Since Joe is nearly always busy with his efforts to extend Mac Dukles into every corner of the globe, Kokie has plenty of time and resources to refine her golf game. She relentlessly pursues perfection in all aspects of her game, taking lessons weekly, reading the latest advice books, and buying every gadget to improve her game. She has a long-game coach, a short-game coach and a putting coach. Her support staff also includes a personal fashion advisor and a golf-focused hairdresser. In spite of all this effort and expense, Kokie has never had a hole-in-one. She contacted me as soon as she spotted a rival winning a few tournaments using my fabulous golf gadgets. Her objective - that elusive hole-in-one!

Kokie first stretches... then hits a few balls.

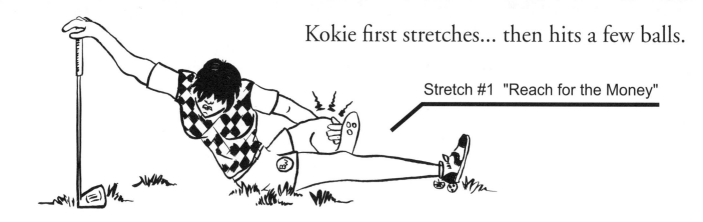

Stretch #1 "Reach for the Money"

Stretch #2 "Corporate Death Spiral"

Stretch #3
"Over the Stock Options"

Driver:
20 Balls...

3 Wood:
20 Balls...

5 Wood:
20 Balls...

et cetera!

Finally, she meditates ... that New Age Financial Meditation.

Kokie will go to any lengths to improve her game. She has scheduled many private meetings with me in my "invention workshop."

Marilee "Mrs. Country Club" Picker

Marilee Picker is a master of the social scene and a fount of gossip. As an LPGA referee for local events, Marilee knows the rules cold. When consulted about a rules infraction (or not) she spouts official rulings straight from the book. Being retired, Marilee plays five days a week and serves on several committees, including the Course Club Advisory Council, the Inter Club Match Bureau, and the Exemplary Henpecker Alliance. She and her husband regularly go on extended golf junkets all around the world. As for the game itself, well, Marilee's game has some rough edges - about 20 strokes worth. My initial reaction was to avoid such a rules hawk in selecting an "average woman golfer." However, I became convinced that her approval for my great golf gadgets would encourage widespread acceptance.

Three swings and some practice putting and she's done. Marilee doesn't want to leave her good shots on the practice tee.

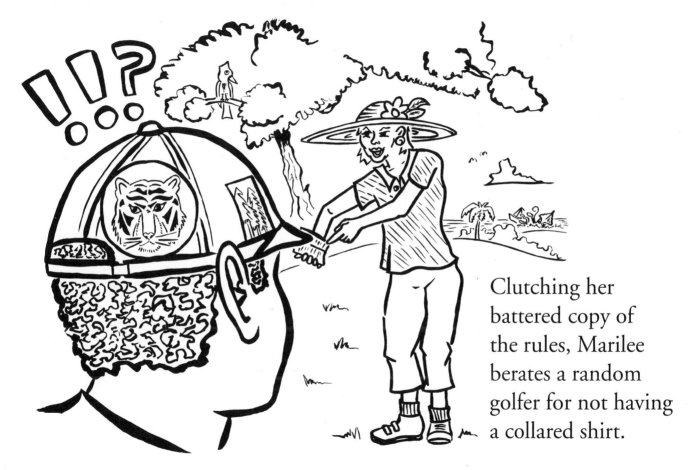

Clutching her battered copy of the rules, Marilee berates a random golfer for not having a collared shirt.

Hole # 1
The Deep Wood

The Deep Wood
Par 4, 257 Yards

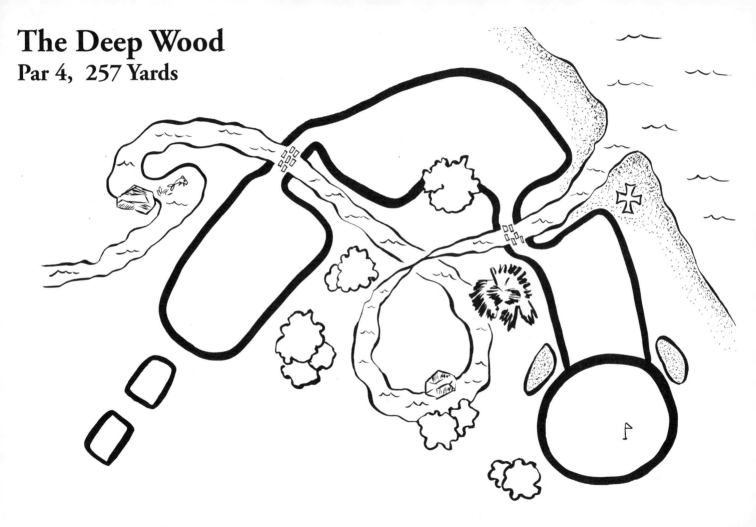

Work on your short game! This hole is pretty easy if you've mastered the art of pitching your ball over narrow obstacles. Two high shots are necessary to get you over the stream that crosses the fairway twice. A decent player can easily reach with the second shot and will putt for birdie. The two things a smart player looks out for on this hole are the deep right rough and the occasional buried treasure on the beach. Let's watch the ladies play this hole.

Jane's shot has way too much left hand.

Marilee is straight,
but not very long.

It looks like Kokie will be in the best position.

Marilee has hit her ball into chipping position and Jane is a similar distance. Just finding Kokie's ball will be the big challenge of the hole!

The Fairway Keen Cutter

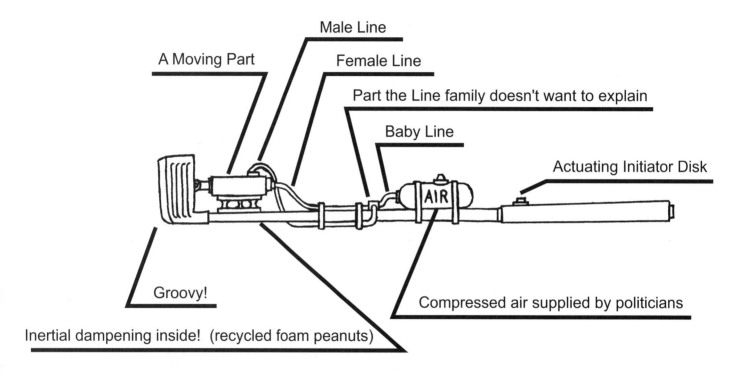

Male Line

A Moving Part

Female Line

Part the Line family doesn't want to explain

Baby Line

Actuating Initiator Disk

AIR

Groovy!

Inertial dampening inside! (recycled foam peanuts)

Compressed air supplied by politicians

The Fairway Keen Cutter is a rather special redesign of the more traditional nine iron. It uses the well-proven technology of the jack hammer. You know those guys that use the heavy, air-driven hammer to cut up concrete and asphalt during rush hour? This blade is much sharper, lighter, and better looking, much like the people who use my gadgets. A little inside-out swing, great for a slight draw, will lift the ball from any lie. Tree branches, OB markers, even rocks can not stop the club head once it is in motion. Look out impediments, Kokie is taking no relief!

The power of this device
can be intimidating to
the unprepared.

She lines up the shot and blasts it toward the green!

I think we can call this invention a screaming success!

Brando's Golf Gadgets: *For Women*

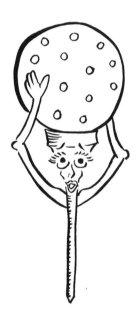

Brando's Golf Gadgets: *For Women*

Hole # 2
Clubbed

Clubbed
Par 5, 510 Yards

A long par five, at 510 yards, this fairway stretches away forever, first with a dogleg to the left, then another to the right. An unexplored swamp surrounded by trees and bunkers lies in wait on either side of the fairway. This hole is a challenge for the best players, and a round killer for many. Be careful! I've had partners go off in search of a ball, and never come back.

Oops! That probably wasn't in her game plan.

Marilee hacks while Jane hunts. This could be a long day for Kokie.

This particular water hazard looks a bit more hazardous than most.

Brando's Golf Gadgets: *For Women*

What a terrible situation! Jane's ball is unplayable, and Marilee is carefully monitoring her 2 club lengths drop. Jane doesn't want to go back to the tee ... that's simply too far. Clearly this is a case for one of my Golf Gadgets!

The Extendo Club

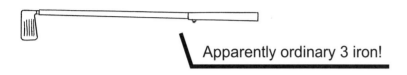

Apparently ordinary 3 iron!

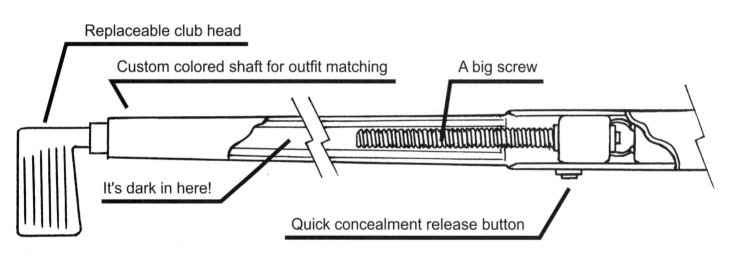

Replaceable club head

Custom colored shaft for outfit matching

A big screw

It's dark in here!

Quick concealment release button

This is a very practical invention for the slightly less-than-perfect golfer. The Extendo Club was made with the understanding that sometimes two ordinary club lengths are just not enough to free the victim from unplayable lies, such as those found on non-fairway surfaces. If the USGA and the Royal and Ancient rules would just be more reasonable about club length, they would quickly see the advantages of the Extendo's construction. Just hold the club level with the ground, and press the quick-release button - the Extendo stretches out to six, twelve, or twenty-four feet, depending on the number of clicks the button is given. Return the club to an upright position and it once again shortens down to thirty-six inches. The result: up to forty-eight feet of "two club lengths."

Jane uses the Extendo Club to take maximum advantage.

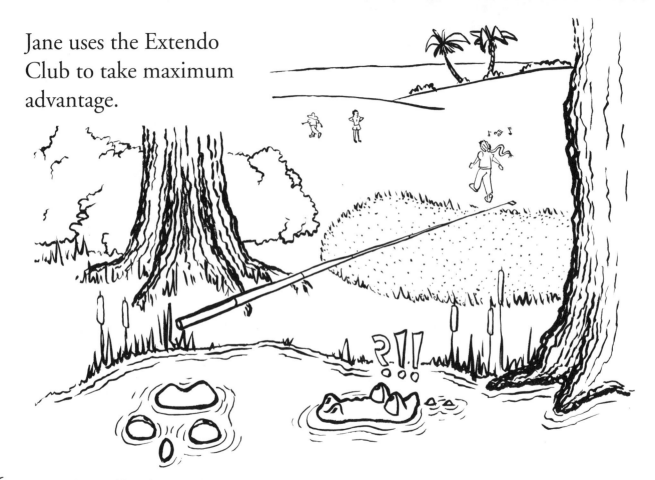

Just look at that!
Back to the fairway,
fair and square!

ZIP

Brando's Golf Gadgets: *For Women*

Hole #3
Put Your Face On

Put Your Face On

Par 3 or 5, 146 or 493 Yards

This hole is unusual in that the par fluctuates from hour to hour. Since the hole winds around the beach, the tide has a big role in determining whether it's a par 5 or a par 3! If the tide is low, an enormous sand bar is revealed. It directly connects the teeing ground with the green and most players treat it as nature's sand trap. In high tide, the player must follow the fairway around the beach, adding at least two strokes to the hole. A tide chart is posted near the tees of this unique hole.

TIDE CHART

While checking the tide chart for the threesome, Kokie finds the timing to be closing in on the par 3, but she decides that they can play it anyway.

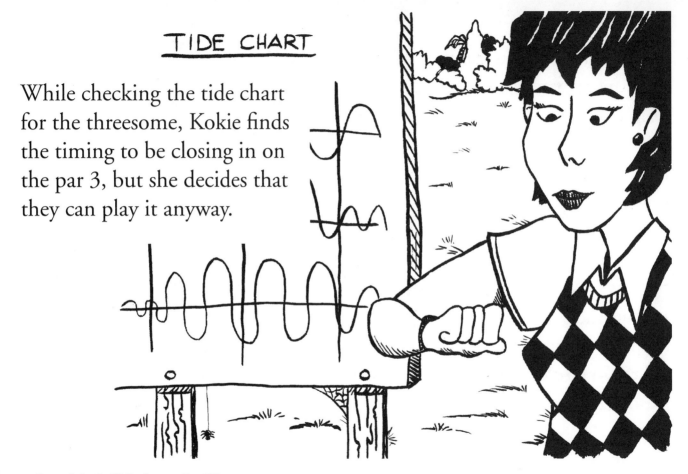

All three tee off and end up on the sandbar.

She appears to be about 60 yards out from here. Jane easily reaches the green with her approach.

Marilee takes over driving duties from her caddy but gets a little stuck!

The caddy vainly tries to free the cart...OH NO! The tide is coming in!

Just like in a school fire drill, Jane orders action!

It's a common miscon-
ception that golf has no
exercise value.

WUMP!

As Jane and Kokie do a little fix-up, Marilee's mirror image is shocking.

Coiffure a la Golf Bag

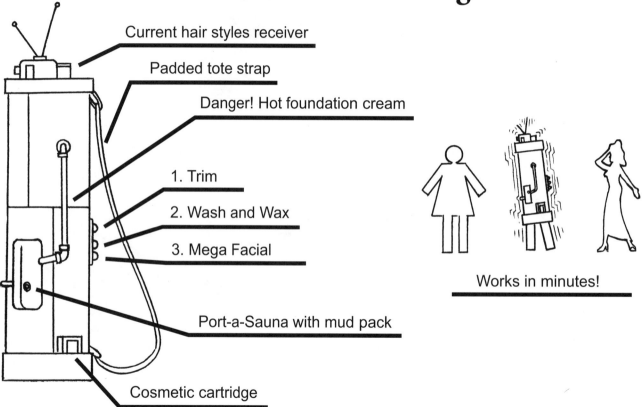

Current hair styles receiver

Padded tote strap

Danger! Hot foundation cream

1. Trim

2. Wash and Wax

3. Mega Facial

Port-a-Sauna with mud pack

Cosmetic cartridge

Works in minutes!

To be frank, the game of golf can be absolutely devastating to a woman's hair! I mean really a mess, and that's not even mentioning makeup. Why has the multi-billion dollar cosmetic industry totally ignored this potential market? I filled this enormous gap with the ultimate in emergency golf cosmetics. The device is named Coiffure a la Golf Bag. To recover your coveted look, simply remove the clubs and place the bag over your head and shoulders. Don't be alarmed! The steam is for gentle cleansing and opening the pores. Dials on the exterior of the bag allow the wearer to indicate summer, fall, winter or spring skin tones for cosmetic harmony. Go ahead and play! The zip down ball pouch allows the wearer to see her next putt as she waits for the Bag to complete its cycle. The Coiffure a la Golf Bag is perfect for the woman golfer!

Marilee chooses Autumn colors and dons the Bag...

... while she comfortably putts for par!

Par in hand,
Marilee removes
the Coiffure
a la Golf Bag.
Success!

Brando's Golf Gadgets: *For Women*

Hole # 4
Clubhouse Duck

Clubhouse Duck
Par 4, 340 Yards

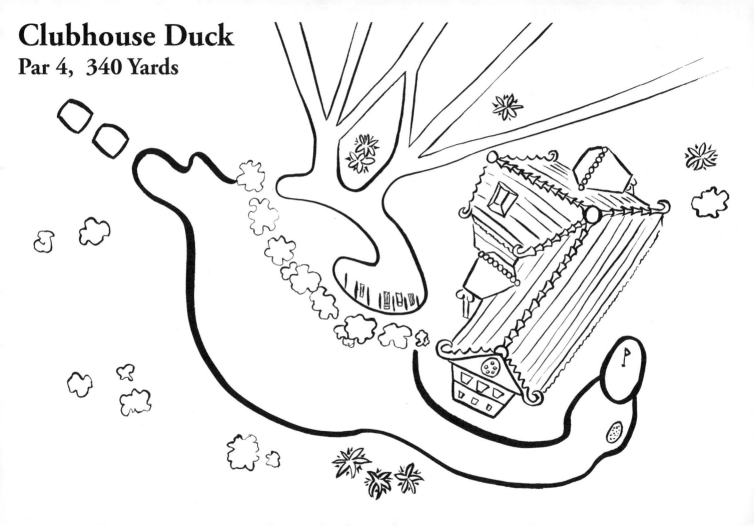

This is one of those holes that make players feel like they are on top of the world. The fairway sweeps gracefully down to the bottom of the hill and then curves gently off to the right. The pin is visible from up here and a trick of the light makes it seem close enough to reach out and touch. The opulent clubhouse lies at the corner bend. The grass is mowed close on the fairway and the earth beneath it resembles concrete. Any ball hit on this hole is likely going to roll forever. It's 260 yards to the bend, and then another 80 to the green. The big challenge for this hole is to ignore the tastelessly overdone clubhouse until the second shot is hit.

Swinging with vigor, Jane hits it long and straight, right for the green... unfortunately the clubhouse is in the way.

The bar patrons get a surprise attack from the east!

For someone without my Golf Gadgets, this would be impossible.

Jane moves the "loose impediments" to clear room for her swing. She'll need my help to get out of this mess.

Superb Angle Finder

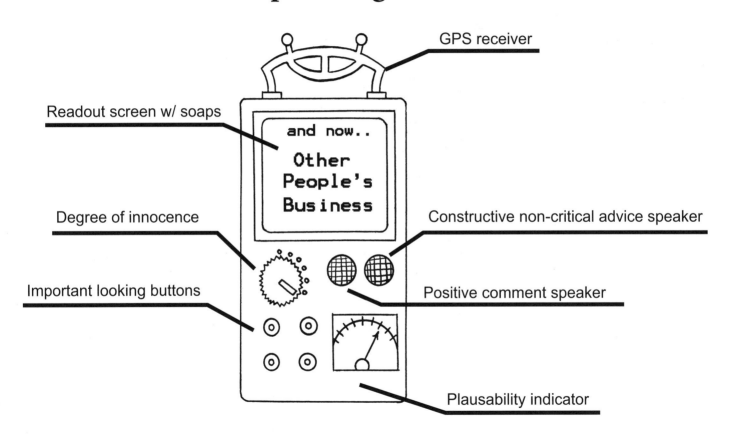

Jane needs my handy Superb Angle Finder, the only gadget for those occasions when the line is blocked by pesky trees, bleachers, or solid oak planks. First activate the device, point the Finder at the ball, then point it at the pin, and that's all it needs! The internal Queasy Logic™ circuits will tabulate the correct angle of attack for your swing. The exact location of aim will be displayed on the screen. Of course, I can make the Finder in many different styles for easy accessorizing with your outfit!

The Superb Angle Finder is activated.

The angle of attack has been determined!

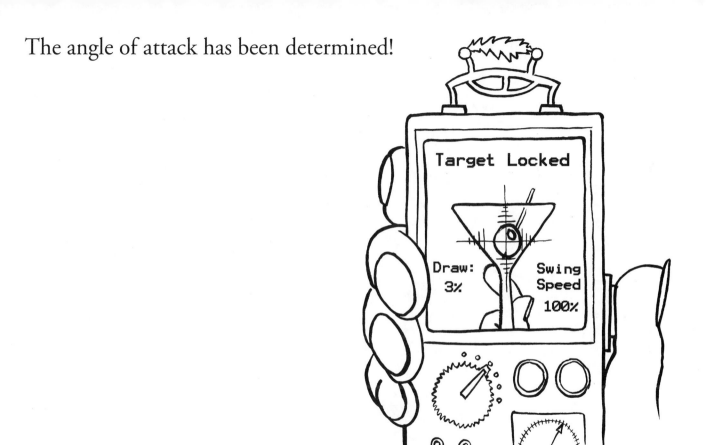

The serenity of golf is legendary!

Well! Jane is hot today. The fourth graders would never recognize their mild-mannered teacher! Hoody Hoo!

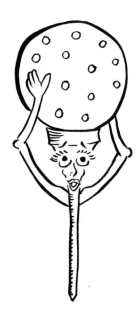

Brando's Golf Gadgets: *For Women*

Hole # 5
Tea Time

Everyone has played at least one hole as boring as this one. The fairway is relatively straight and level. It's a 340 yard par four. Bunkers are predictably placed, one on each side of the green. The trees are evenly spaced along the fairway with military precision. In an attempt to appear interesting, the hole itself is four inches to the right of the exact middle of the flat green. How do these get into the course design? Did the architect go on vacation to the Big Island while the Army drew up some plans? However it happens, that's the hole. I'm snoozing!

The tee shots are predictably average.
Enthusiasm runs high.

Marilee takes her next shot...

Maybe it's time for a break and a light snack. You know, even five holes is too far to go without refreshment! These ladies are bored with this hole - a granola bar and a bottle of water aren't enough to elevate their enthusiasm. To provide a little gustatory diversion, I came up with plans for the ultimate food-service solution!

The Tea Times Rolling Service

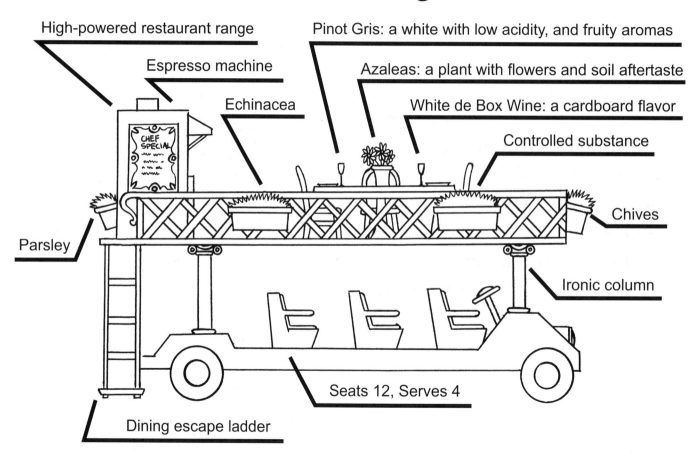

High-powered restaurant range

Espresso machine

Echinacea

Pinot Gris: a white with low acidity, and fruity aromas

Azaleas: a plant with flowers and soil aftertaste

White de Box Wine: a cardboard flavor

Controlled substance

Chives

Parsley

Ironic column

CHEF SPECIAL

Seats 12, Serves 4

Dining escape ladder

The Tea Times Rolling Service was extremely difficult to design for a number of reasons. It had to serve at least four, and what about the dessert course and champagne chiller? It goes without saying that it also had to be practical and quick on the course. The finished device is one hundred percent pure rolling elegance, but can whip up a gourmet lunch without slowing up play. Anybody ready for lunch?

Marilee orders the salmon crepes, Jane orders some grilled mushrooms and onions with cream sherry, and Kokie a plate of steamed vegetables with a side of wasabi and ginger.

During the second course, Jane excuses herself momentarily to go hit her ball.

The chef garnishes the delicate flan with carmelized raisins and then sets it on fire.

The Tea Time Rolling Service! It's the ultimate answer to those Cravings de Bore (hunger due to boredom).

Brando's Golf Gadgets: *For Women*

Hole # 6
Kokie's Correction

Kokie's Correction
Par 4, 345 Yards

Kokie has always had problems with this hole. Whether it was too many swing thoughts or that the air was heavy that day, Kokie has never birdied this hole. If you even mention the word "choke" within a hundred feet of this fairway, she'll be on you like a tigress. No amount of golf tips or expensive outfits have helped her with this beast. Maybe it's the elevated tee that's throwing off her sense of distance, or perhaps it's that feeling of impending failure on the hole. Whatever it is, we'll see if one of my golf gadgets can remedy the situation. It's a Par 4 at 345 yards, with a water hazard and sand traps.

Kokie tees off with her usual commitment to style.

Despite Kokie's excellent form, she has put her ball right in the lowest point in the fairway. From here, she cannot even see the pin!

The Simplified Swinger

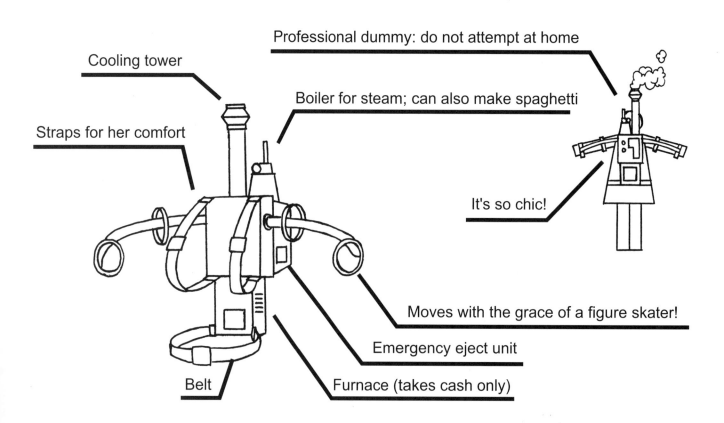

Professional dummy: do not attempt at home

Cooling tower

Boiler for steam; can also make spaghetti

Straps for her comfort

It's so chic!

Moves with the grace of a figure skater!

Emergency eject unit

Belt

Furnace (takes cash only)

This is a gadget that simply leaped into my head one day on the course and, a mere three years later, it only needs a few more improvements to make it commercially viable (aka, safe for humans). Anyway, the Simplified Swinger is the answer to your target golf needs. It is a swing trainer that goes the extra mile for your game. The golfer enters the location of the target into the device and then securely straps it on. The machine then guides your hands gently but firmly along the ideal swing plane. Some naysayers claim that this means you aren't playing the game, but we all know that they only bring up this weak argument after they've lost a few rounds to this gadgeteering brilliance. All the golf literature tells you to play smart golf! Well, my friend, using this gadget is so smart it takes your game out of your hands while the club is still in them! Shock your opponents with the Simplified Swinger!

Kokie has entered the target co-ordinates into the Swinger and is now ready to start it up. Jane wisely dives for cover.

WUMP!!

Wow! Watch the
Simplified Swing
in action!

The Simplified Swinger makes shot making as smooth as glass.

Brando's Golf Gadgets: *For Women*

If I can just work out some minor bugs, this gadget will be ready for the tour in no time!

Brando's Golf Gadgets: *For Women*

Hole # 7
Stone Froufrou

Stone Froufrou
Par 3, 83 Yards

This hole has its green right in front of the Clubhouse. It's a short par three framed by stone statuary and ornamental hedges. The green is somewhat narrow and surrounded by deep traps in front and on the right. Of particular note on this hole, the famous Italian artist Michael D. Angelo has contributed one of his more popular works, *Ode to the God of Golf*, which is displayed prominently in front of the clubhouse. It is said that if the God winks at a player, she will break a hundred on the round! A hundred clubs, that is.

Jane's tee shot doesn't look good. Maybe it's part of her plan.

Jane asks Marilee about relief from the statue. Unfortunately, rules are rules. She cannot move that ball!

The Irrepressible

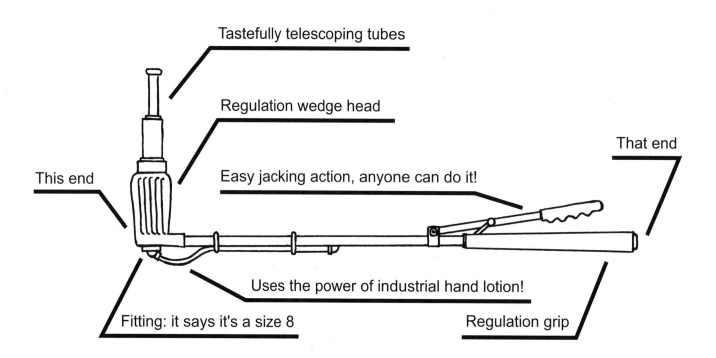

Tastefully telescoping tubes

Regulation wedge head

This end

Easy jacking action, anyone can do it!

That end

Uses the power of industrial hand lotion!

Fitting: it says it's a size 8

Regulation grip

W e've all had this problem. The course is very pretty, but the layout provides too great a challenge - at least for our game? The greenskeeper must have a diabolical sense of humor! The hundreth time this happened to me, I dropped everything and headed for the workshop. Five days later, I had achieved the brilliant Irrepressible device. It will give relief from statuary, boulders, and even larger obstructions. It also functions as a wedge, so the player does not have to break her timing by going back to her bag. A simple flop shot over the newly cleared space and a par is possible!

Whoa! It's her or the lawn sculpture!

The Irrepressible
is unstoppable!

The God of Golf is now a pile of rubble and can't stop Janes's beautiful chip shot.

Some may resent your resourcefulness.

Brando's Golf Gadgets: *For Women*

Hole # 8
Personal Summer

Personal Summer
Par 4, 365 Yards

This hole is of medium length and major difficulty. The tee shot goes over a huge ravine and uphill. Then the fairway bends to the right and rises again to a two-tier green. Trees line both sides of the course. An ornamental lake welcomes those who are long and left off the tee. Curiously, millions of dollars worth of golf clubs are found at the bottom of the ravine every year. To capitalize on this large natural deposit of titanium, I have been working on an automated golf club retrieval system. I'm still in the design stage.

While Jane has hit a decent drive, Kokie has a bit of a problem with hers.

Marilee hits one short, but right down the center!

Kokie hits a three wood out of the rough on the left... into the rough on the right.

Marilee makes another short but competent shot.

Jane puts three balls in the lake from the same spot! Though quite consistent, she decides she's had enough fun on this hole. She does not want to buy more balls at the turn.

Kokie blasts one into the greenside bunker!

Marilee's eclectic swing yields greenside territory!

Away, Kokie displays deft technique in getting out of the bunker.

As Marilee approaches the par putt, she suddenly begins to feel warm. No one else is feeling the heat, it must be a personal summer!

Just when you need to concentrate on that critical stroke, biology has to make a statement. It may be a pleasant 68 degrees for them, but suddenly it's 114 for you. The sweat goes down your face and your game goes down the tubes. It's evident that this problem is yours and yours alone. That's why women need my Hot Flash Suppressor!

Hot Flash Suppressor

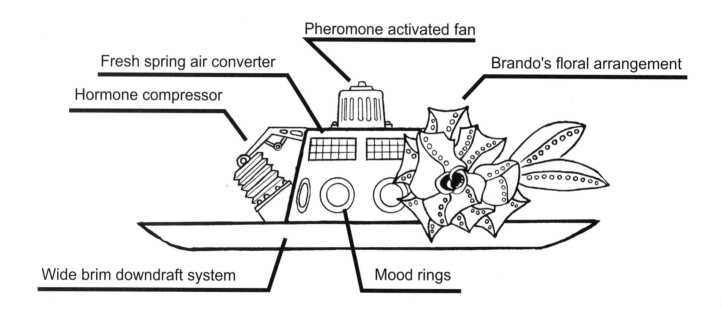

Pheromone activated fan

Fresh spring air converter

Brando's floral arrangement

Hormone compressor

Wide brim downdraft system

Mood rings

The Hot Flash Suppressor is guaranteed to cool you down while your game heats up. It conditions the air in order to make it literally cooler around the wearer. I call this new process "air conditioning" and I expect it to have quite a few applications in the golf world. The force of the air movement is adjustable and includes a humidifier option. My lawyer was trying to suggest another name... something about copyright infringement. I think the invention stands on it's own!

Marilee dons the Hot Flash Suppressor and prepares to putt.

Marilee sinks the putt to win the hole!

Brando's Golf Gadgets: *For Women*

Hole # 9
Down the Garden Path

The Garden Path
Par 4, 375 Yards

This fairway is parallel to the previous one. A par four with a big dogleg right. It has a left rising slope and further down, right rising slope. Three bunkers surround the green. There are relatively few trees on this hole and the land is more open. This part of the course runs along the nation's only golf-winged butterfly preserve. These rare insects are distinctive and come in several varieties. There is the High Spin, the Soft Feel, and the Ladies Solid Core subspecies as well as many others. They are quite social with other butterflies. Social butterflies are often seen on golf courses.

It's a beautiful day to be on the course. Listening to the roar of the butterflies, Kokie, Jane, and Marilee move off the tee to their second shots.

What is that!?

O.U.T.F.I.T.
(Opulent Units of Tightly Folded Instawearable Textiles)

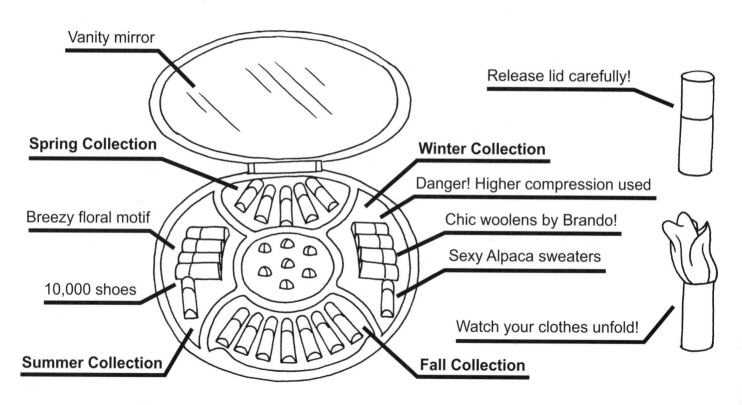

Vanity mirror

Release lid carefully!

Spring Collection

Winter Collection

Danger! Higher compression used

Breezy floral motif

Chic woolens by Brando!

Sexy Alpaca sweaters

10,000 shoes

Summer Collection

Watch your clothes unfold!

Fall Collection

Imagine catastrophe. Secure in your impeccable sense of fashion, you confidently venture forth for a wonderful day of golf. After playing a few holes in your usual brilliant manner, seeing and being seen, you languidly gaze off into the fine afternoon haze. You suddenly realize that SHE IS WEARING MY OUTFIT!!! Imagine the incredible gall of the woman! Someone might think you're copying HER! What is a girl to do? It's times like these that my friends reach for O.U.T.F.I.T. Yes, it's the answer to life's most trying fashion questions - and it fits in your hand. With the selection of a cylinder the wearer can assume a wide variety of current trendy styles. Dozens of choices are available in easy to open canisters of super compacted outfits. Modern micofibers make wrinkles a thing of the past. Just open, shake out, and put on your dream ensemble!

The first option is a classic black evening gown, perfect for a night on the town. But, not appropriate for here.

Option #2 is very comfortable... for the beach!

Ah, Option #3 gives her the ultra modern look. Very nice!

Saved from a major fashion gaffe by the O.U.T.F.I.T.! The others move on while Kokie fires her fashion consultant.

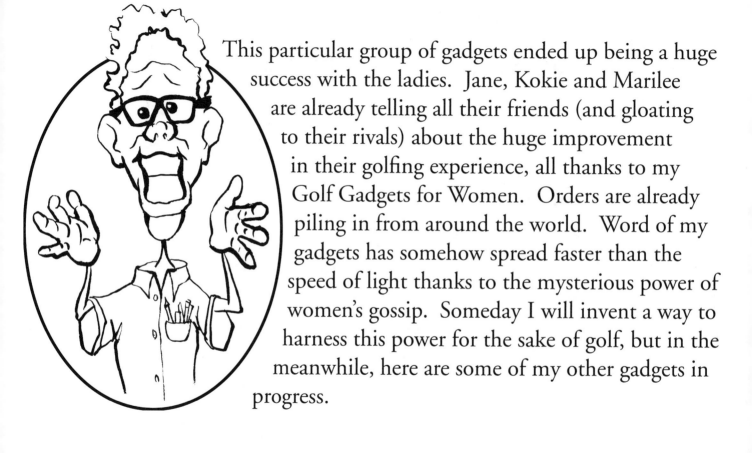

This particular group of gadgets ended up being a huge success with the ladies. Jane, Kokie and Marilee are already telling all their friends (and gloating to their rivals) about the huge improvement in their golfing experience, all thanks to my Golf Gadgets for Women. Orders are already piling in from around the world. Word of my gadgets has somehow spread faster than the speed of light thanks to the mysterious power of women's gossip. Someday I will invent a way to harness this power for the sake of golf, but in the meanwhile, here are some of my other gadgets in progress.

Miniature Maintenance Men

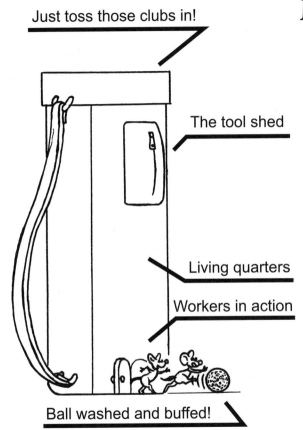

Just toss those clubs in!

The tool shed

Living quarters

Workers in action

Ball washed and buffed!

As any gadget needs some regular maintenance, I trained this team of highly dedicated and intelligent field mice to properly clean and maintain the various golf gadgets I have invented. When not doing mechanical work, these industrious mice will even set up your tees for you. Unfortunately, I have been running into some problems with their union, but I expect negotiations will go faster after I buy a cat.

The Equalizer

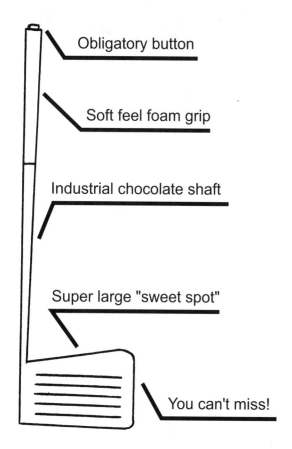

Obligatory button

Soft feel foam grip

Industrial chocolate shaft

Super large "sweet spot"

You can't miss!

In order to level out the inequality in the sizes of men and women's golf clubs, I designed this new wedge. After power injecting a mold with industial chocolate and leaving it out for several months, I discovered an incredibly tough and resilient material for this device. This tool gives women all the size they ever wanted in a club. Club pros say it's not really the size of the club that matters, but the motion of the swing. Now you can decide for yourself!

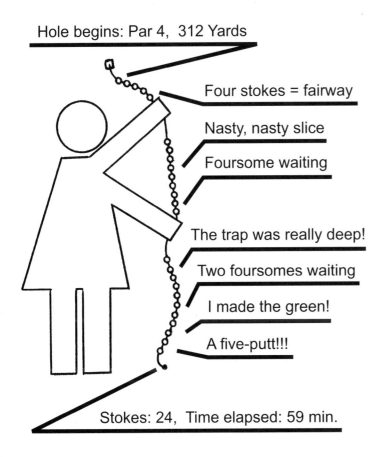

Hole begins: Par 4, 312 Yards

Four stokes = fairway

Nasty, nasty slice

Foursome waiting

The trap was really deep!

Two foursomes waiting

I made the green!

A five-putt!!!

Stokes: 24, Time elapsed: 59 min.

Brando's Beads

Those stroke counting beads are a very handy item and many women wear them on the course. But do they really work for the par challenged? The average bead string is just not up to those 23 stoke holes! That's where Brando's Beads come into play! Sporting 25 beads on a four foot lanyard, it's the solution hack masters have been looking for. It's the accessory that says, "My scores are amazing!"

Brando's Golf Gadgets: *For Women*

The End

I am an inventor and strive to solve all of golf's dilemmas by designing special gadgets. I am preparing my next round of golf gadgets to reduce your score a few more strokes. If you have any golf problems requiring a solution, devices to be engineered, or golf situations for which you need an escape, feel free to e-mail me at gbrobst@gebcoeng.com. Device or scenario descriptions become the property of Sonoma Publishers. You can't take a tax deduction for the contribution, but you will get your name in print.

- Brando

Dan Frazier is definitely whacked. It can probably be attributed to a childhood spent talking to farm animals in California, or possibly it can be blamed on his father, the ex-NASA rocket scientist that sells car insurance. Either way, his arts are unique by default (one way or the other). This is not his first book, although his children disagree.

Gary Brobst is a man pushed to the wall by pressures within the nuclear power industry. Firstly, it is mind-numbingly boring, and secondly, no one wants to be around if it gets exciting. Forced into finding other work, Gary has fallen into the poverty-generating trade of writing and publishing humor books. This is not his first book. Someday, he hopes to go back to calculating zinc deposits and giving seminars in Nebraska, but until then he will continue to think of new ways to play golf.